Process Intelligence

FOR

DUMMIES®

SOFTWARE AG SPECIAL EDITION

by Tobias Blickle, Helge Hess,
Joerg Klueckmann, Mike Lees, and
Bruce Williams

Foreword by Dr. Carsten Bange

WILEY

Wiley Publishing, Inc.

Process Intelligence For Dummies,® Software AG Special Edition

Published by
Wiley Publishing, Inc.
111 River Street
Hoboken, NJ 07030-5774
www.wiley.com

For general information on our other products and services, please contact our Business Development Department in the U.S. at 317-572-3205. For details on how to create a custom *For Dummies* book for your business or organization, contact bizdev@wiley.com. For information about licensing the *For Dummies* brand for products or services, contact BrandedRights&Licenses@Wiley.com.

ISBN: 978-0-470-87620-6

Manufactured in the United States of America

10 9 8 7 6 5 4 3 2

WILEY

About the Authors

Dr. Tobias Blickle is Director of Product Management for Process Intelligence at Software AG. Dr. Blickle studied Electrical Engineering in Saarbrücken and received his diploma in 1993. His PhD on Evolutionary Algorithms was awarded with the prize medal of the Swiss Federal Institute of Technology Zurich in 1996. He has published several articles about Process Intelligence.

Dr. Helge Hess is Senior Vice President of Product & Solutions Management at Software AG and has over 20 years of experience in the consulting and software business. In parallel to different management positions within the product division, he was in charge of IDS Scheer's BPM Consulting and Academy for some years. Dr. Hess graduated from the Universität des Saarlandes in Germany with an MSc in Computer Science and was a fellow of the Studienstiftung des Deutschen Volkes. He obtained his PhD in Economics and was the recipient of the Dr.-Eduard-Martin Award from the department of Business Administration for his research concerning the reusability of software components. He is a frequent speaker at BPM conferences and events and has written numerous articles and co-authored books about Business Process Management, Process Intelligence, Performance Management, and Organizational Analysis.

Joerg Klueckmann is Director of Product Marketing for Process Intelligence Solutions at Software AG. He studied Sociology, Business Administration, and Intercultural Communication at FSU, Jena, Germany, and LSU, Baton Rouge, USA, graduating with distinction. Prior to joining Software AG, he was Head of Product Marketing at Intershop and IDS Scheer. He has written numerous articles about Business Process Management, Business Innovation, and Process Intelligence.

Mike Lees is Vice President of Enterprise BPM Solutions at Software AG and was previously responsible for the BPM Business Line at webMethods/Software AG. Prior to joining webMethods he was Founder and CEO of the market-leading metadata and knowledge management vendor Cerebra, Inc., which was acquired by webMethods in 2006. He has held senior positions in technology analysis and fund management organizations. Michael is a qualified UK Chartered Accountant

(ACA) and has a degree in Business Economics from Durham University, England. He is co-author of *BPM Basics For Dummies.*

Bruce D. Williams is Senior Vice President and General Manager of Strategic Programs for Software AG and was previously the Vice President of BPM Solutions for webMethods. He has graduate degrees in Engineering Computing and Technical Management from Johns Hopkins University and the University of Colorado and a BS in Physics also from Colorado. Bruce frequently writes and speaks on topics about business and technology trends. He is co-author of *Six Sigma For Dummies, The Six Sigma Workbook For Dummies, Lean For Dummies,* and *BPM Basics For Dummies.*

Dedications

Tobias Blickle: To my family.

Helge Hess: To Anette, Jana, and Henri.

Joerg Klueckmann: To my parents Baerbel and Gerd.

Mike Lees: To those I love.

Bruce Williams: To everyone with the vision and dedication to unite process improvement with information technology.

Authors' Acknowledgments

The authors acknowledge Nancy Beckman, Mike Burns, Ruth Ann Femenella, Aleksandra Georgieva, Kevin Iaquinto, Bryan Quinn, and Annette Rebellato for their guidance and assistance in the preparation of this work.

We thank Wolfram Jost, Susan Ganeshan, Markus von den Driesch, Frank Gahse, Andreas Kronz, Ricardo Passchier, Matt Green, Andrea Nygren, Patrik Hachmann, Andreas Koch, Winfried Barth, Michael Timpe, Marie-Elisabeth Kuppler, Harry Enns, and Ian Walsh for their support in the development of the book.

Table of Contents

Foreword

. . . .

*P*rocess Intelligence is the answer to the organization's need for timely process information and the ability to make the rapid decisions demanded by today's dynamic economic developments.

Traditionally, business intelligence concepts focused on internal and external reporting. Most notably, data warehouses were developed in the early 1990s to provide integrated and consistent data to support management decisions. At about the same time, technology for On-Line Analytical Processing (OLAP) started to gain mainstream adoption to enable end-users with fast, interactive analysis of their business data. Both concepts form the foundation of many Business Intelligence systems today but are limited to report on information from the *past*.

Ten years later, around the year 2000, there was a growing understanding that the collection and creation of strategic planning data reflecting an organization's *future* is also an important part of Business Intelligence. Planning was added to reporting and analysis applications that mostly reported on the deviations between plan and actual data.

Now in 2010, the unpredictable and ever-changing economy also forces organizations to look at the *present*. Processes are now under closer scrutiny and need to be monitored and analyzed in real time to enable organizations to react more quickly to business events. Organizations also want to automate decision making when possible during process execution. Process Intelligence systems offer a solution to this by combining the technologies for monitoring past and present performance, planning support for the future, and supporting the immediate operational needs of processes.

Both from a conceptual and technological point of view, the emergence of Process Intelligence has just begun. Research at the Business Application Research Center (BARC) shows that many organizations lack the fundamental prerequisites to be in a position to implement Process Intelligence. This starts with defining and measuring Key Performance Indicators for processes and ends with the implementation of the necessary technology, for example, the ability to quickly integrate and analyze business process data. But the need to integrate Process Intelligence into Business Intelligence and process management strategies will grow quickly, so it is essential to start looking at it today.

This book provides a good starting point for companies that want to adopt the concepts and technology for Process Intelligence. It provides an excellent overview on Process Intelligence concepts and technology and will help you to take the first steps into an exciting new chapter of Business Intelligence and decision support. I hope you enjoy reading this book and wish you every success in implementing its ideas.

Dr. Carsten Bange
Founder and CEO
Business Application Research Center (BARC)

Introduction

*I*t's a process world. In 21st-century business, you must have a process-oriented view of your enterprise. You must have access to process information and make it comprehensible and applicable because the very essence of business performance is based on the effectiveness of your processes. Hundreds or even thousands of processes are active across your business enterprise; how well you understand and manage them defines your success.

To excel in this environment, you have to have more than just an education and some skills. Those will get you started, but you need to be process-smart and process-aware. Even process smarts aren't quite enough, though. You have to be instantly up-to-the-minute knowledgeable. And even with all this, you've got to be able to apply this process savvy with insightful reasoning and goal-directed problem-solving ability.

Putting all this together means you need to have intelligence in a process-driven enterprise. In other words, you have to have *Process Intelligence*.

Process Intelligence has quickly emerged on the business landscape as the way for people to excel in the modern process-oriented world. Process Intelligence is a well-designed and engineered set of tools and techniques for understanding an enterprise from a process perspective, characterizing active processes, and knowing what's happening within and around them.

About This Book

We wrote this book as a primer and as a reference for you. You may be a business manager, or an IT practitioner, or maybe an ambitious career individual who wants to know what Process Intelligence is and how to apply it. This book is for you!

Process Intelligence For Dummies, Software AG Special Edition is more than just an overview or survey of Process Intelligence. It describes both the business management and information technology sides of the story and delves into the process-centric foundation upon which Process Intelligence is built. As a basics book, it is necessarily brief, so you'll want to follow up in some of the areas that are most interesting or important to you. This book is also a reference book that's organized into chapters, so you can flip right to what you need.

We use some business management, process improvement, and information technology concepts and language in this book. To get extra smart on some of these aspects, check out *BPM Basics For Dummies* by Kiran Garimella, Mike Lees, and Bruce Williams; *SOA Adoption For Dummies* by Miko Matsumura, Bjoern Brauel, and Jignesh Shah; *Six Sigma For Dummies* by Craig Gygi and Bruce Williams; and *Lean For Dummies* by Bruce Williams and Natalie Sayer. Also check out *Balanced Scorecard Strategy For Dummies* by Charles Hannabarger, Frederick Buchman, and Peter Economy (all published by Wiley).

Icons Used in This Book

In the margins of this book, you will see some helpful little icons that can help you pinpoint particular types of information:

Key points for implementing Process Intelligence successfully.

Caution — a risk or pitfall could get you into trouble.

When you see this, it's an indication of a technical detail.

This is where we've summarized a concept for you.

Chapter 1

Get Smart about Process Intelligence

*P*rocess Intelligence is a special combination of savvy and information. You learn the savvy part through education, training, mentoring, and continuously applied experience (refer to Chapter 4). The information part is captured and brought to you by information systems and technologies (see Chapter 3 for more on this). These systems are part of the information infrastructure of your business. They're also part of the information universe that includes systems within the businesses of your customers and suppliers, and even other information and systems out across the Internet.

Process Intelligence satisfies your hunger for knowledge about your business by feeding you the information you need, anytime you need it, in the way you can digest it and turn it into energy going forward.

Understanding Process Intelligence

Process Intelligence is the ability to understand business processes and knowing how to use them effectively. When you *have* Process Intelligence, you can *use* your business processes to improve product and service quality, productivity, and profitability by making process information more accessible and comprehensible, and then directly applying it to your business activities. Process Intelligence is a cornerstone of Business Process Excellence (BPE), enabling you to better leverage your investments in management methods, information systems, and technology infrastructure to improve operational performance at every level and more precisely execute on your strategic intent. In short, Process Intelligence helps to adjust and apply your processes to compelling business advantage.

Process Intelligence assists everyone involved in a process to make better decisions every day — including process engineers, managers, operations folks, and technical staff. Process Intelligence includes technologies that use intelligent software to enable better and faster reasoning about process data. Process Intelligence software applies sophisticated tools to tasks such as knowledge acquisition, data analysis, system control, and process optimization. Process Intelligence tools gather process data, provide interpretations, and make both historic and real-time results available across your enterprise and even to your suppliers and customers.

Process Intelligence is enabled through technologies and practices that are the culmination and evolution of tools like Business Intelligence (BI), Business Activity Monitoring (BAM), and Process Discovery, combined with analytical methods like Six Sigma, and enabled through Business Process Management (BPM) solutions. In Process Intelligence solutions, the technologies are seamlessly integrated, rapidly deployed, and easy to use, leading to dramatic improvements in business performance.

With Process Intelligence, you can

- ✔ Discover opportunities for savings by seeing precisely where waste and loss is occurring in your business

- ✔ Know immediately when a business process, activity, or transaction encounters a delay or commits an error

- ✔ Uncover weaknesses and areas of exposure in any part of a process or activity

- ✔ Understand the connections between high-level strategy and operational activities

- ✔ See the how value streams between you, your customers, and your suppliers are working

Because Process Intelligence is so powerful, you can apply it to any business process or function. People use Process Intelligence for everything from order processing, service management, transaction banking, sales, insurance, health care, energy and utilities, logistics, and more. In a process world, everyone seeks Process Intelligence.

Outcomes like revenues, profit, and customer turnover are the visible results of the many intermediate activities and events within a business. Figure 1-1 paints the picture. Countless influencers lurk beneath the surface of your business to affect these outcomes. Of the many operational activities and business processes active in an enterprise, what's the connection between these few *lagging* financial indicators and the many *leading* process-oriented indicators? When you have the ability to understand these connections, interpret the leading indicators, and derive the proper immediate concrete actions to improve your results, you have Process Intelligence.

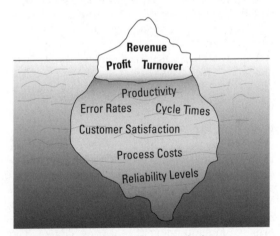

Figure 1-1: The tip of the performance iceberg.

Process Intelligence is sought by every corporate manager so they can effectively interpret operational Key Performance Indicators (KPIs) in the context of their real-world business processes. You want process efficiencies and operational performance to be transparent at all times. If your KPIs aren't where you need them to be, you want to immediately identify and resolve the anomalies. People can't wait until the end of the quarter, the end of the day, or sometimes even another ten minutes to know whether the factors influencing their targets are on track. With Process Intelligence, you can constantly check how all the pieces of your enterprise are performing. Replace crisis management with the intelligence to correct errors before problems become serious.

Tools of the past, such as traditional Business Intelligence (BI) software, are too cumbersome and time-consuming. They don't allow you to see the direct link between KPIs and the end-to-end processes causing these indicators, or immediately take action to improve your business processes and outcomes.

Making the Process-Driven Organization a Reality

Successful process-driven organizations share a sense of purpose and priority. They can translate strategy into action, define the key indicators of performance at every level within a coherent hierarchy, and manage the processes that drive performance. Successful enterprises can synchronize their long-term strategic goals with the everyday tactical execution of their related processes. And they accomplish this by applying Process Intelligence.

Intelligence is power

With Process Intelligence, you can assess your business processes in terms of speed, cost, quality, quantity, and other key measures, and turn your business into a higher-performing enterprise. You have the power to continuously adjust and improve the way your internal and external business processes perform. By understanding KPIs as they happen in live business processes, you can make objective decisions and realize your improvement potential. Just imagine the impact you can have by easily identifying the factors that impact process effectiveness, and by discovering and reusing best practices.

What's in it for me?

You aren't born with Process Intelligence, and you don't just suddenly wake up one day with a towering process IQ. You develop your process knowledge and analytical capabilities over time. And what do you get as a result?

- ✔ **Better performance**: Improved processes lead to improved business performance; you're more competitive and make more money.

- ✔ **An efficient early-warning system**: Get out from under reactive responses by seeing critical key indicators of performance (quantity, time, cost, quality) in real time — or even predict potential outcomes.

- ✔ **Faster and better decisions**: Identify process deficiencies more quickly, and take immediate corrective action before things get out of hand.

- ✔ **More with less**: Get more out of your people, time, and money by reducing waste and eliminating mistakes in how work gets done.

- ✔ **Informative benchmarks**: Understand what's happening now. Benchmark your processes so you know where to apply improvements and best practices.

Developing Process Intelligence is the best and fastest way to achieve these benefits. But you don't have to train to become a Six Sigma Black Belt or hire a bevy of programmers to make this happen! The methods and tools of Process Intelligence are now available to everyone.

The Three Levels of Process Intelligence

Orient your perspective on processes according to three levels: strategic, tactical, and operational, which naturally align to three classes of stakeholders: strategic, tactical and operational.

The strategic stakeholders

The senior-most managers need easy-to-interpret KPIs that deliver relevant facts to help them make informed decisions.

Strategic stakeholders need to answer questions like:

- ✔ Where are we now, relative to plan?
- ✔ What's working? What isn't working?
- ✔ Will we achieve our goals?

Top managers respond best to visuals like dashboards, so they can assimilate information easily. For them, Process Intelligence is how all the tactical and operational processes roll up to these top-level outcomes. A view that provides interactive traffic lights, trend charts, and deviations from planned performance levels (such as time, cost, quality, quantity, risk) is what managers need in order to understand the status of their performance-driven organization.

The tactical stakeholders

Process owners need end-to-end detailed information. They must ensure process efficiency and effectiveness — which they can only achieve by continuously monitoring whole live processes and evaluating them in terms of quantity, time, cost, quality, and risk.

Process owners seek Process Intelligence in order to rigorously analyze their processes — even down to a single instance. An average process cycle time of 6 days from ten processes might be caused by two of the processes needing 10 days while eight processes needed just 5 days. Process owners must be able to find out what causes the two processes to need 10 days. After identifying the root cause, they can then address the causes and fix the running processes.

What tactical stakeholders want to know is:

- ✔ Where do we need to intervene?
- ✔ Are our interventions, changes, and improvements working?
- ✔ What further changes do we need to make?

Looking just at the KPIs won't identify the nature of weaknesses and areas for improvement. You have to see and understand the structure of your processes and find out which activities are performed, in what order, who is involved, and what's happening. Every individual process instance can be processed in its own way, so you need to see each process instance and have the ability to examine the precise details to discover the real issues.

You don't learn much from looking at averages. You need to see the whole landscape — the ranges, the distributions, and the individual instances. Most often, it's the outliers that drive your overall performance, so be sure you see the big picture.

The operational stakeholders

The largest group of stakeholders is the operations staff. They need to know what's happening within their individual work processes right now, in real-time, on an event-by-event basis. They also need to know where they stand in the end-to-end value stream. People in operational roles need to manage current transactions and respond to critical issues as they happen. They need the knowledge of incoming events and downstream results, and to be aware of critical situations in a way that frees them to perform their work but also to respond to important exceptions and take immediate action. The operational stakeholders seek answers to questions like:

✔ How well is everything working right now?

✔ What's going wrong? What action should I take to fix it?

✔ What's coming next? What do I need to be ready for?

Truly understanding a process isn't simple. Gaining the insight needed for Process Intelligence takes time and skill. Managers need to ensure the operations staff have the support and assistance they need to be successful "process engineers."

The Cycle of Business Process Excellence (BPE)

The continuous cycle of improvement, may be a phrase you've heard again and again. But you've heard it many times because it's important. Take a moment to examine the life-cycle diagram in Figure 1-2.

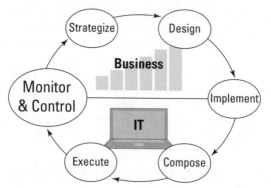

Figure 1-2: The life cycle of Business Process Excellence.

You can't have one without the other

Everyone used to look at improvement cycles as being contained within either a business area or confined to the IT world. But these days, you can't do one without the other. Process improvement life cycles are part business and part IT, and there's a synergy in how they work together. Figure 1-2 shows the lead responsibility lies with the business, but it's collaboration between business and IT, all the way through.

Staying on point

Life-cycles go round and round, but change isn't really supposed to be constant. Just like the rest of us, processes need stability, too. The result of process improvement is in achieving a point of stability; you then stay on point to monitor and control the improved process. That's why this phase appears largest in Figure 1-2. Process Intelligence lives at this point of performance. During the improvement life cycle, you must design-in the intelligence capabilities (See Chapter 4), but you apply Process Intelligence most as you monitor and control.

Chapter 2

What Process Intelligence Can Do for You

*O*nce you can see your enterprise from a process perspective and have the intelligence to really know what's happening with your business processes, you can boost performance in every corner of the enterprise.

Think Process — See Process

Process Intelligence is partly in the ability to think about your business in process terms and partly in the ability to see those processes in action. You have to grow beyond what we were all taught to do, which was to think in functions and look for outcomes. And you have to really see your processes — in all their depth and detail, in aggregate and in pieces, individually and connected — to gain the insight and have the intelligence to know how they affect your business.

If you haven't been exposed to process-centric business models, you're in for a change. Look up some of the references on process management in Appendix B to better understand what Business Process Management is all about.

Process Intelligence gives you the ability to distinguish what's wrong from what's right. Once you set a limit, a threshold, a goal, or a boundary condition for any Key Performance Indicator (KPI) on any process, it's clear from that moment forward whether the process is misbehaving.

- ✔ When a process is behaving, you want the comfort of knowing everything is all right.
- ✔ When a process is misbehaving, you want to know *everything* about what's gone wrong.

For this reason, most of your focus in Process Intelligence is around understanding what's happening when things go wrong, so you can take corrective action.

Black Box and White Box: Two Views of a Process

Process Intelligence enables you to understand both the external and the internal workings of a process. The *external* or *black-box* view of a process tells us about the process: how the process is interacting with the outside world and how it is performing as a member of the value stream. The *internal* or *white-box* view of a process reveals its inner workings and enables you to detect critical failures and make fast adjustments down to a single instance.

Knowing about processes

Everyone must have constant up-to-date information about performance in their area of responsibility. This includes the people who are stakeholders in the performance of tactical and operational process, along with the process owners. Process Intelligence provides an objective performance assessment of the business: speed, cost, quality, quantity, and risk, and identifies areas for improvement. Two classes of insight are:

✓ **Quantitative,** based on the measurement of objective end-to-end process indicators

✓ **Qualitative,** based on graphical or organizational representations of the process structure

Seeing inside processes

Operations staff need to know what's going on within a process, as it's running — as people are performing, systems are processing, material is flowing, energy is consumed, and transactions are processed. Sometimes, they need to know down to the tiniest level of detail, for a single instance, and at a single moment. They need immediate visibility, context, and insight and the intelligence to make proper decisions instantly.

Process Intelligence Revealed

Process Intelligence is something you develop. It isn't something you hire. It's not performed by a consultant and delivered in a report, nor is it something you outsource to have built for you. And it's not something you buy in a box. You build your Process Intelligence by understanding the fundamentals of process behavior and with the assistance of tools and technologies that deliver you information.

The time when consultants would walk through the company, interviewing the employees and retrieving performance indicators by hand is over. "How long do you take to file a tender typically?" "How many invoices did you process last hour?" Business is more digitized, and information within and about processes is available through IT.

Doing as-is before to-be

It's always tempting to dismiss current difficult conditions as the old way of working and to focus energy and attention on developing new and better ways. It can seem like a waste of time to spend any effort on what people may agree are broken processes. But don't run away so quickly.

You must first understand the as-is state. Every day is the as-is state.

You must have insight and understanding of your as-is processes because if you don't, you don't know where the problems are and what to "fix." You may unwittingly throw away perfectly good things. Furthermore, if you don't effectively characterize your current condition, you won't know the value of the changes you've made when you're done!

Knowing that you don't know what you don't know

Unless you effectively characterize your present as-is state, experience shows that teams tend to focus on the main activities and the most desired paths and omit the less common activities and paths, in order to reduce their overall effort. This type of modeling can at best provide only a rough understanding of the process because it isn't detailed enough to support a real implementation. At worst, it misses key sub-processes, paths, and conditions.

Insufficiently modeled processes miss critical process conditions. In order processing and servicing, these include:

- ✔ When orders are unexpectedly modified by the customer
- ✔ How orders are split apart by a supplier (due to delivery bottlenecks)
- ✔ The way customers complain about invoices and service
- ✔ When incoming payments are partial, or missing, and reminders are necessary

Because these various events occur in the real world, you need Process Intelligence to really understand what happens. Knowledge about the actual structures and execution of each process instance is indispensable. You'd want to know things like:

- ✔ When and how often are orders modified?
- ✔ How often and in which scenarios are orders split?
- ✔ What were customers complaining about?
- ✔ How many reminders were necessary until the customer accepted and paid invoices in full?

Only with full knowledge of the as-is condition do you know to ask these questions and design this intelligence into your to-be state. Without this knowledge, you just don't know what you don't know.

Perhaps the single greatest barrier to adopting Business Process Management has been in the challenge of properly modeling a business process. Unless you're trained and experienced, process modeling can be somewhat of a mystery. It's easy to get off-track and model poorly — whether you're modeling the current as-is process or designing a new one.

Process Intelligence tools help you hurdle this barrier with ease. They have the unique and innovative capability of discovering existing processes *automatically* and generating a graphical model of process instances. Furthermore, the results display precise details of this particular case and enable evaluation and analysis.

True Process Intelligence provides a view into every process instance — capturing and visualizing them automatically. This bottom-up approach lets you instantly calculate the benchmark indicators for true root-cause analysis.

Discover and visualize single process instances

Automated Process Discovery (APD) tools can extract and characterize all process-relevant data and events from your IT systems (such as ERP, CRM, middleware, workflow engines, legacy systems, and such). APD constructs a visualization of each executed process instance (such as: *show me customer order 12345 from May 5th at 10:37 a.m.*). For simple process executions, the reconstruction shows a sequence of activities and functions, called an Event-driven Process Chain (EPC). For complex processes, process constructions include graphs with branches and junctions. For each process instance, the result is a perfect image of reality, using standard notations.

You're now naturally thinking: That APD sounds like a miracle. But it's true you don't have to model the process in advance. You identify the measuring points and connect to the systems, and APD generates the model and a series of process steps.

Discovering aggregated process views

For high-volume processes, don't try to analyze each single process instance separately. Instead, aggregate the individual instances of processes into a collection. You may then identify that you want to be informed only about certain conditions. Process Intelligence technologies will aggregate these processes and search for conditions (such as: *all standard orders received last week from customers in the west region with an order value above $12,000*) and will deliver a graphical representation of the aggregated processes plus the KPIs for the selected request (see Figure 2-1).

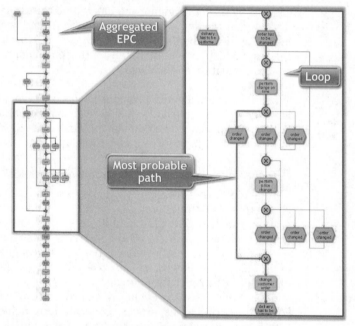

Figure 2-1: Aggregation of process instances.

A Process Intelligence tool will dynamically generate an aggregated process view for each query and compare and benchmark the behavior of different variables, for example, departments, plants, regions, and so on. By drilling into details, such as a low-performing region, you get a detailed picture of the behavior of the organization and can compare it to the behavior of high performers — thus identifying the best practices in your organization.

How does this work? To generate a graphical visualization of an aggregated process, objects and connections that fulfill equivalence criteria are combined to form one object or connection. The logical workflow sequence is retained by incorporating connectors (AND, OR, and XOR branches) in the process work flow sequence. The visualization of the discovered model then becomes the basis for a structural analysis of the process because it shows the most important paths and activities in the process.

With advanced visualization techniques, you can gain further insights.

- ✔ **Probabilities** of various paths are expressed graphically by different thicknesses of the connections.

- ✔ **Paths** below a certain probability threshold can be hidden.

- ✔ The **layout** can be arranged automatically according to the most probable execution path.

- ✔ **Function symbols** can be colored according to KPI values.

- ✔ **Trends** and traffic lights can be shown to visualize the performance (cost, processing time, and so on) of activities.

Process Intelligence provides the process owner with the perfect combination of instruments for process analysis and optimization:

- ✔ Identify (and color code) weaknesses (extended processing times, high costs) and potential for optimizing the process flow.

- ✔ Analyze probabilities in the control flow and identification of critical paths and exceptions.

- ✔ Understand how resources (teams, groups, and so on) are allocated to activities.

Furthermore, you can see the structure as a Gantt chart to comprehend easily the sequence and overlap of activities in the process (see Figure 2-2). This is especially useful if you're looking for waiting times within a process.

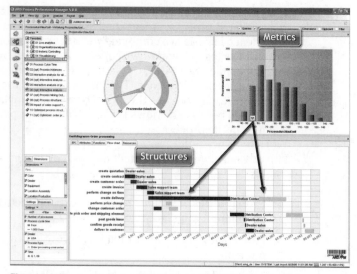

Figure 2-2: Aggregated visualization as a Gantt chart.

Automated organizational discovery

As if discovering processes automatically isn't exciting enough, Process Intelligence tools can discover organizational relationships. After all, if you need to optimize business activities and analyze processes, you need a behind-the-organizational-chart view. See Figure 2-3.

In many scenarios, analysis of the team structure and paths for cooperation are more important than analyzing the process structure in detail. With organizational discovery, you can visualize the actual collaboration between teams and departments within the enterprise.

Organizational Discovery (OD) uses techniques derived from statistics and sociology, including Organizational Analysis (OA). Using this approach, users can identify who is performing a particular task, how often, and with whom, as well as their response and throughput times.

Similar to process discovery, OD uses data from the underlying IT systems to examine the real-world relationships between teams and groups. In this environment, *relationship* can mean collaboration, delegation, informing, reporting to, reviewing, and so on. In addition, this approach shows which processes an organizational unit is involved in and for which parts of a process it is responsible. Visualizing these relationships is an important requirement for identifying, analyzing, and optimizing actual communication during process execution.

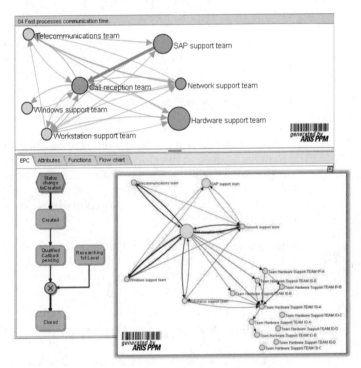

Figure 2-3: Automated discovery of organizational structures.

The intelligence sought from organizational discovery includes:

- ✓ Which organizational units and entities perform which activities? How often? What level of quality is achieved? What are the throughput times or delay times?
- ✓ Which units work closely together?
  - How often do different organizational units work on the same process instance?
  - How often is work passed between organizational units?
  - Where do bottlenecks arise?

✔ Which employees and entities act as the communication paths to other departments? Who has specialized knowledge?

✔ How busy is a department? How can personnel costs be cut?

✔ Who delegates to whom?

When it comes to optimizing corporate efficiency, you want to really understand the teams that are engaged in the processes and workflows. In particular, you want to examine post-merger integrations, restructuring projects, new employee on-boarding, personnel development, assembly of project teams, and working with partners outside the organization.

In many large companies, communities of practice often come into being — even at the global level — which are very significant for knowledge-sharing and innovation. By examining the patterns and roles, you can apply metrics that identify teams that act as central connectors in a group of companies or as peripheral specialists.

The highest-performance teams and employees aren't necessarily the result of the greatest individual expertise. Often, performance results from a significantly diverse network of contacts, both within the company and outside it.

Indicating performance — KPIs

After you've recognized your as-is processes through automated process discovery, you can determine which performance indicators are key to understanding their behavior. Key Performance Indicators (KPIs) are the metrics that help you truly characterize processes. They're the measurement points that reveal the inner workings of the processes that drive your business.

KPIs come in two flavors:

✔ **External:** Customers and suppliers see you from the outside. For them, KPIs include time, quality, price, and service levels.

✔ **Internal:** Inside your enterprise, the focus is on the effectiveness of processes. Internal KPIs include volume, cost, risk, and resources.

Refer to Figure 2-4 for more about KPIs.

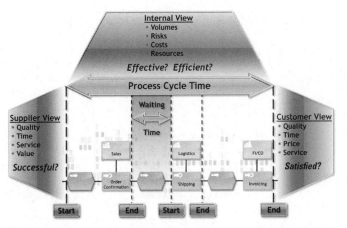

Figure 2-4: Internal and external perspectives on process performance.

KPIs have attributes, dimension, and hierarchy. They're also *dynamic* — changing in value over time. Your Process Intelligence derives directly from the ways you define your KPIs, so that you can analyze, compare, trend, correlate the information properly to the process, and draw the right conclusions. Refer to Figure 2-5.

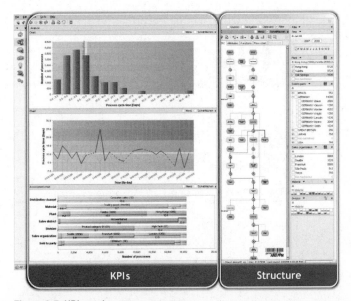

Figure 2-5: KPIs and process structure.

Getting to the root cause

With the help of process discovery, you build a model of your as-is processes. And with a healthy selection of KPIs, you have metrics and measures that indicate process performance. Now comes the fun part: getting to the root cause of what's driving internal and external performance.

Usually, you begin measuring process performance at a high level of abstraction — something like a display board with dials and signal lights. But what's causing these outcomes? For example, why has the signal light indicating cycle time gone from green to yellow? This step is where you drill down into the causal elements.

When analyzing root cause, follow the path from performance indicators to both process structures and organizational structures. This combination is especially important in obtaining a meaningful analysis of bottlenecks.

Process Intelligence technologies, such as data services for extracts and data mining, as well as analytical tools and display systems, are all part of your root-cause analysis (see Figure 2-6). Beginning with the KPIs, you utilize these technologies to reveal the internal structures and critical combinations and patterns that describe the behavior of the process.

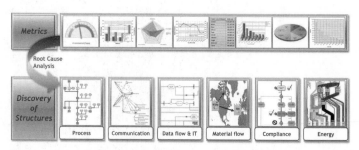

Figure 2-6: Root cause analysis from metrics to structures.

Analysis techniques from approaches like Lean and Six Sigma come in handy when looking for root causes because they provide methods and tools for determining the causes of process outcomes. These include fishbone diagrams, CT (critical to) trees, cause and effect (C&E) matrices, Pareto analysis, failure mode effects analysis (FMEA), and a variety of statistical analysis tools. Having Process Intelligence means you will naturally utilize these tools.

Rolling it all up

After you've discerned the root causes of what's driving the key performance outcomes of your process, you've boosted your Process Intelligence to an advanced level. Congratulations! You're now able to answer all the fundamental questions you need to apply your knowledge to action:

- **What are the results?** What are the KPIs — the outcomes of our processes?

- **How were the results produced?** What were the process steps taken that generated these outcomes?

- **Who was involved?** What was the organizational structure and contribution to these processes?

- **Why did this happen?** What caused these outcomes?

Benchmarking

Use your Process Intelligence to benchmark process performance against goals, markets, and competitors. You can also compare scenarios. Benchmark processes per each KPI:

- Compare indicators relative to one another (such as throughput time or process costs in Region A versus Region B).

- Compare performance of a process relative to its structure and how effective that structure is in delivering key outcomes (such as complexity and structure of processes in Region A versus Region B).

You can see an example of Process Intelligence benchmarking of best practices between two regions in Figure 2-7.

These comparisons can lead directly to discovering the weaknesses and failure modes within the processes. In Figure 2-8, you can see where benchmarking enables you to find the slow spots.

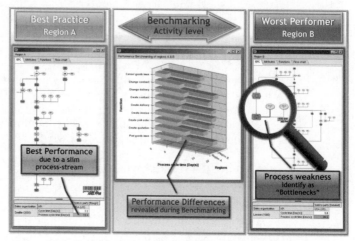

Figure 2-7: Comparison of two regions using benchmarking.

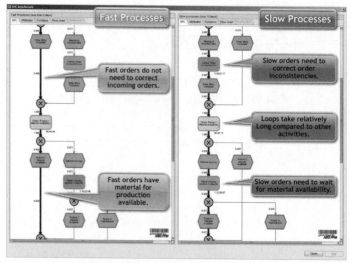

Figure 2-8: Using benchmarking to find weaknesses.

Intelligence Capabilities

Your Process Intelligence attaché case contains many additional capabilities beyond the basics. You have 21st-century tools at your fingertips that dramatically enhance your intelligence capabilities. These include dashboards, mashups, real-time event processing, alerting, and predictions. These are the keys to real power!

Dashboards and mashups

Process Intelligence requires the fast and easy assimilation of large volumes of information. It has to be easy to interpret and deliver the relevant facts to support rapid understanding and decision making. You have to be able to see different combinations and views of both internal and external processes and KPIs; you have to see them in the context of your immediate situation; the information needs to be a combination of text and graphics, with colors and charts. This is what *dashboards* and *mashups* do for you.

Performance dashboards

With a performance dashboard, you combine the enterprise process landscape with a visualization of associated KPIs. This combination enables people to immediately identify deviations from planned values. Performance dashboards also enable people to drill down to the desired level of KPI detail. See Figure 2-9.

You can filter data by time, region, product group, and so on, and can use indicators like traffic lights and trend charts to show deviations from planned values. With fast access to current, decision-relevant data, you can also easily analyze specific aspects of business performance.

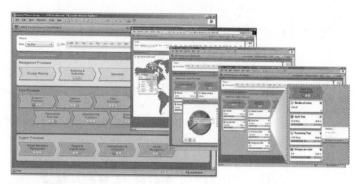

Figure 2-9: Performance dashboards.

The purpose of a Process Intelligence dashboard is to provide information quickly and concisely and present it in a clear and attractive way. People need intuitive views of all relevant information — and they need to adjust their view quickly and easily.

Mashups: Unlimited combinations

Mashups are one of the more exciting recent developments in Process Intelligence. Historically, people struggle to find information and generate reports and dashboards quickly and in an attractive and appropriate graphical form. Organizations invest millions of dollars creating reports that people ultimately never read. Mashups can make information much more relevant and exciting.

Mashups are a revolutionary new capability that enable people to easily create and manage their own graphical dashboards, based on any particular situation or task of interest. The term "mashup" in the music world means a blend of existing content to create something new. This kind of blending is now possible in the world of Process Intelligence.

Mashups are being widely embraced by the IT community. Mashup technology leverages the principles associated with Service Oriented Architecture as defined in Appendix A, utilizing services that access and reuse existing content. Standard interfaces support loose-linking of different resources, with operators for aggregating, filtering, sorting, and mixing. And mashups aren't just for Web content; company data can also be integrated, from application packages like ERP and CRM, to data warehouse systems and file-based information. And the info can be delivered to any type of platform.

When creating a mashup, you take process performance information from just about any source, combine it, and aggregate it into a regular information feed. Mashups integrate the feeds with graphical visualizations, and, *voilà*! You end up with a custom performance-oriented dashboard in a matter of minutes. Figure 2-10 is an example of a mashup, created in just this manner.

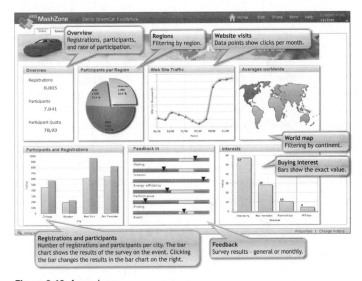

Figure 2-10: A mash-up.

Fast, faster, real time!

Business pressures and technical capabilities continue to accelerate the pace of business activity. Businesses today demand lightning-fast response times, whether in regard to financial transactions, processing logistics, managing customer relationships, complying with legal requirements, or some other metric. We're on our way to a world where information, decisions, and action all occur in real time.

Think of how fast things are moving already:

- ✔ Flight and hotel reservation systems display up-to-the-minute details of available options and process orders immediately.

- ✔ Loans are approved or rejected online in minutes.

- ✔ Customers can make purchases at online stores instantly — and are also offered other, related products just as quickly.

- ✔ News is available on your mobile phone.

To be able to run your business in this lightning-quick manner, you have to monitor operational business processes end to end, extract data, and analyze results on demand. The new technology that links this rapid analysis directly to operational processes is called *event processing*.

Complex Event Processing (CEP) is a capability you use to analyze transactions automatically and respond to critical events in real time. With CEP, you can monitor millions of events continuously, identify critical situations, and take action. Not only is this extraordinary capability something ordinary people can't do themselves, but with CEP, people don't have to burn themselves out trying. Having CEP in place reduces risk, improves response to errors and outages, and helps you beat the competition.

Danger, Will Robinson!

Solid intelligence means you have a high sensitivity to danger. Process Intelligence means you're quickly alerted to problems and issues in your business processes. Whether something's late, lost, broken, or stuck, if it's in the danger zone, you'll know. That's because your Process Intelligence toolkit includes *alerts*.

Alerts are signals that something's gone wrong. They may be visual, audio, mechanical, or personal. Alerts cover the range from a simple notification of a low-level problem, a warning of a midlevel problem, or an alarm of a significant problem.

A fundamental capability of your Process Intelligence means that anyone can have the ability to know when something's not going according to plan. Then, with today's technologies, alerts can be channeled just about anywhere. You can receive an e-mail on your computer; you can receive a text or page on your mobile phone; you can have sounds and graphics jump on your screen and you can have notifications sent to many people who will converge on you to be sure you know!

Oh — and alerts can be for nice things, too. "Your coffee's done."

Predicting the future

Part of intelligence is intuition: the sense that something's going to happen. Process Intelligence has this sense, too. That's because Process Intelligence can collect enough history and observe enough behavior to know when certain events are likely to follow certain others.

Through a mathematical inference algorithm based on Bayesian statistical processing, the event of a past failure can be recorded — as well as the conditions of all causal contributors. As the pattern of those causal elements repeats, the algorithm can predict with a calculated statistical confidence level the probability that the event will occur again.

Process Intelligence or process prescience? When you're able to know that something's about to go wrong with enough time to prevent it, you've got both.

Chapter 3

The Information Architecture of Process Intelligence

*T*he data and processing systems for Process Intelligence are designed, assembled, and applied in special ways to bring you the process information you seek, and to analyze, arrange, and present it to you when you need it, and in just the way you need it. This chapter explains these systems in greater detail.

The Process Intelligence Information Architecture

The information architecture for Process Intelligence is a Service Oriented Architecture designed to fit as part of an overall Business Process Management (BPM) solution. Figure 3-1 is the information architecture model of BPM (Refer to *BPM Basics For Dummies*). Note that the elements that support Process Intelligence are a naturally integrated part of BPM.

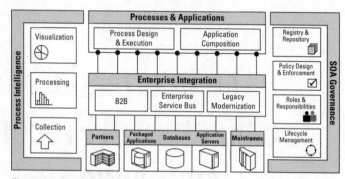

Figure 3-1: The information architecture model for BPM.

You can see the three major components of the Process Intelligence information architecture in this model: collection, processing, and visualization. You can also see why Process Intelligence is so effective, because it is well-connected to all the goings-on in the information world. Nothing escapes the eye of Process Intelligence! And, you're able to connect back directly from your intelligence work to effect action via systems of management and control.

Process Intelligence information is collected, processed, and delivered for consumption by your strategic, tactical, and operations staff. But Process Intelligence isn't an offline activity. It's not as if massive data collection systems are just scraping up gobs of information and shoveling them into a big processing machine for analysts in a dark room to ponder on giant monitors, hoping for moments of *Eureka!* In fact, it's exactly the opposite of that: Process Intelligence is tightly integrated at all levels and engaged in the real-time comings and goings of process information, so everyone can to use it continuously as an integral part of their regular business activities.

You can imagine that the collection, processing, and visualization technologies of Process Intelligence are kept pretty busy. After all, nearly one zettabyte of digital data is being generated *per year* on a global basis (in case you're wondering, a *zetta-byte* is a nearly incomprehensible 10^{21} bytes!). The internal architecture of Process Intelligence (see Figure 3-2) is designed to manage large volumes of information for consumption by a widely distributed audience across all levels and geographies. However, Process Intelligence is mainly intended for individuals who are managing or performing within business processes. It gives them the ability to sense and respond to events and circumstances *as they're happening*. As a result, the information architecture of Process Intelligence is both robust on its own and is also a part of BPM.

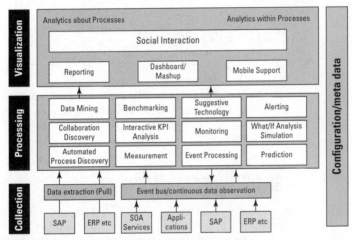

Figure 3-2: The IT architecture of Process Intelligence.

The Process Intelligence architecture includes technologies like operational business intelligence (BI), Complex Event Processing (CEP), and Business Activity Monitoring (BAM). These technologies are a departure from the traditions of analyzing historical data offline. Instead of just looking backward at what's already happened, Process Intelligence also monitors live processes with the purpose of helping you take appropriate action before problems materialize. Technological advances, such as replacing conventional database systems with efficient in-memory technologies, virtualization, and Service Oriented Architectures (SOA) make this possible.

The rest of this chapter takes an in-depth look at each of the three layers of the Process Intelligence IT model.

Process Intelligence Collection

The whole point of Process Intelligence is to understand process information faster and more easily. Chapter 2 describes how Process Intelligence involves both knowing about processes and knowing what's inside them. To accomplish this,

Process Intelligence technologies monitor events in order to know about processes, and they extract data for analysis to know what's happening inside them. These two approaches are known as data extraction and data observation.

Data extraction

With *data extraction,* you retrieve data from databases and systems that support the business processes. Typical applications include ERP and CRM systems. Process Intelligence extractions may fetch large amounts of data at once, in order to gain the insight needed about the performance of a process or processes.

Data observation

In *data observation* mode, you're simply watching and monitoring activities in the IT universe. The architecture accomplishes this through loosely coupled applications and services, connected via a common information layer, or *bus,* using a SOA architecture. This way, you can support real-time interactions and detect complex events using a Complex Event Processing engine (refer to Chapter 2). Data observation is especially useful because the global information architecture is becoming more service-enabled and event-driven.

In the real world, information about processes doesn't come from a single source. You have to be able to get information from multiple sources and in multiple ways. Your Process Intelligence architecture must help you get the information you need from any source — quickly and easily.

Process Intelligence Processing

Process Intelligence processing sculpts buckets and jumbles of information into powerful intelligence. You can access this intelligence through the visualization tools (see the next section), and you can feed the results via Services into your BPM engine to control processes directly. Processing is the most complex part of the Process Intelligence information system, with 12 different subsystems. We describe some of the more important ones here.

Process and organizational discovery

Process and organizational discovery is the capability to generate a process from uncorrelated events. Each instance of a business activity is captured, and the process is assembled automatically. The process flow is generated in real time, on the fly.

Process discovery is a complex task. Thousands and even millions of steps are extracted from different systems and are matched in real time to keep the process instance current. Because the extracted data isn't necessarily in order, the discovery process is internally complicated. If not done right, the result would be a jumbled mess of bad information.

Although process discovery is a complex and difficult task, it's a critically important part of Process Intelligence. The challenge of process definition is one of the greatest barriers to adopting Business Process Management (for more on this, see Chapter 2). Process discovery capability is therefore one of the most powerful elements of Process Intelligence.

Event processing

Event processing sets the rules and conditions for detecting specific events and then generating the information and outputs that enable both people and systems to respond appropriately. An advanced form, known as Complex Event Processing (CEP), addresses the larger challenge of detecting a pattern based on many events and correlating them, analyzing the impact, and then recommending action. Process Intelligence emerges as users can understand larger issues that emanate from individual processes.

Alerting

Alerts are notices when exceptions occur. You can set limits for any metric or KPI in any process. If the value of the metric ever breaches the limit, you're alerted. An alert can be as simple as an e-mail or as complex as triggering a new business process using the event bus or SOA infrastructure.

Prediction

Prediction uses Bayesian statistics to determine the probability of future events based on past behavior. Prediction will *snapshot* the value of all KPIs whenever an out-of-limits condition is detected on any metric. If the same metric moves out of limits again, prediction will snapshot all the KPIs again and examine the two sets for correlation. This process is repeated again anytime the metric goes out of limits. After a statistically valid correlation is established, prediction is able to forewarn you of an impending out-of-limits occurrence to within a measured degree of statistical confidence.

All the events monitored and detected by CEP are stored in process and KPI storage areas. Process Intelligence technologies are fully capable of dealing with millions or even billions of data sets and process instances.

Interactive KPI analysis

Sometimes, you just want to examine a single measure or performance indicator and quickly understand what's happening. With interactive KPI analysis, you can select any measurement item and perform analysis, such as comparisons and dependencies, right there in real time. An interactive analyzer looks for outliers, so it's easy to find the trouble spots or outstanding performers and determine what's causing them.

Benchmarking

What if you need to make comparisons? *Benchmarking* lets you compare multiple processes and scenarios against one another and output the results. You may also want to compare against industry standard benchmarks from institutions like the Supply Chain Council or the American Productivity & Quality Center (APQC).

Benchmarking lets you compare two outputs or KPIs for processes with different characteristics — such as the throughput time for the same process running in different offices. With benchmarking, you can also examine the process structure and compare it to another region or industry standard (see the example in Chapter 5).

Simulation

In many cases, you want to test a process before unleashing it in the real world. *Simulation* lets you create what-if exercises and examine the outcomes. Simulation takes a process or organization model and lets you run through it with test data; you can also run real data from an old process through a revised process. Either way, you get to experiment.

You can adapt simulated process models to individual needs, including the attributes of the modeling objects. This can be useful for specifying things like times and costs, defining the frequency of process execution, or deploying different resource allocation strategies. You may also want to allow stochastic or random values — for instance, when defining function execution times or using rules to manage process maps. This lets you see the dispersion effects that often occur in reality.

Even with the wide variety of settings available, simulation runs are quick and easy to execute because the settings are easy to adjust. You can simulate as-is processes without changes, in order to verify your model. Then you can gradually test the adjustments.

Process Intelligence Visualization

After all the data collection and information processing, the intelligence still needs to get into your head. Until we have mind probes, this last step is best accomplished by creating visuals — charts, graphs, pictures — as the best ways for you to really grasp the full breadth of information. It has been long understood that visuals are the most powerful way to absorb complex information. That's why we have so many charts in this book!

Graphical *dashboards* with *mashup* technology allow just about anyone to build interactive graphical views of processes. They take KPIs generated from data out of the processing layer from real-time information (as well as historical data) and present it in ways that are well suited for your needs.

Social interaction is becoming more important as users want to interact and share content. The idea of community is part of your Process Intelligence — to emphasize the role of the user and to increase the spread of knowledge about processes and performance across a company and its value streams.

Chapter 4

Developing Your Process Intelligence

· ·

· ·

*Y*ou're not naturally born with Process Intelligence — the ability to reason about processes, to think abstractly about them, to comprehend complex process ideas, and to plan to solve process problems. Process Intelligence is something you develop — continuously, through knowledge and experience, combined with ready access to information. You develop the knowledge part with training and experience. You augment that knowledge using technology, which you implement as an enabling platform in a phased approach.

Learning about Process

Everyone knows something about process. For example, you may get up in the morning, have breakfast, get dressed, and find your way to work. That's a process. It's also a process with variation: Some days you may be better at it than others. It's a process with defects: Some days the alarm clock doesn't go off. It's a process with an outcome: You get to work so you can earn a living. And it's a process with Key Performance Indicators (KPIs): getting up, completing your meal, dressing, and arriving at work. And don't forget root causes, such as getting to bed on time the night before, having clean clothes to wear, or remembering to put gas in the car. Everyone innately knows these basic things about process.

Applying this type of thinking to your work processes isn't a big leap, but it is a bigger effort to learn the rigor of defining and characterizing, then analyzing, improving, and controlling your work processes. Getting a Six Sigma Black Belt, for example, usually begins with having an advanced degree and years of experience in a field like industrial engineering. Black Belt training takes a full three months, plus an implementation project and a peer-reviewed report-out. Then there's the experience gained from multiple projects in different areas of discipline. But a Six Sigma Black Belt is like a PhD in process; most people don't need that much process knowledge!

Process basics

The purpose of a business process is to transform something in a way that creates value. A process is the way you take some set of things — information, materials, and/or conditions — and create an outcome of greater value. A process consumes time and resources, and you know you have a successful business process when you've generated a net value greater than the cost of the resources used in the transformation. Meanwhile, because countless things are always lurking that conspire to doom the process to underperform, you need to have visibility and control to help ensure the process keeps generating value.

Processes can be simple (stock a shelf) or complex (change out the landing gear on the Space Shuttle), but both types are based on the same fundamentals. The science behind business processes stems from the industrial revolution of the early 20th century and is now applied most often using methods like Lean and Six Sigma. Regardless of the methodology, it all boils down to this: How effective are you in using a process to create value?

Six Sigma

The most popular method of process definition and improvement is Six Sigma — the quality initiative first developed by Motorola in the 1980s. Six Sigma teaches you a standard way to define a process and then how to measure and analyze it to characterize its effectiveness. Next, you learn how to design improvements to the process and then finally, how to control it to adhere to your improved design.

Although Six Sigma can be applied to extremely complex processes, it can also be very powerful for ordinary business processes. You can be trained to any of several levels of knowledge in Six Sigma, which are designated in belts, like in martial arts, beginning with White Belt, then Yellow, then Green, and ultimately Black. You can learn a lot about process through training in Six Sigma.

Lean

Another way you can learn about process and process improvement is by learning Lean. Like Six Sigma, Lean is based on the same industrial science developed by the original quality masters: Shewart, Deming, and Juran. But although Six Sigma is very problem-focused (fix this broken process now!), Lean is more continuous and incremental (improve your process a little bit every day).

Lean practice was first developed in Japan, so when you learn Lean, you learn to use many Japanese terms, like *Kaizen* (everyday improvement), *Gemba* (where value is created), and *poka-yoke* (mistake-proofing). You also learn to study the process deeply, watch it carefully, and come to know it intimately. Only this way can you really know how to improve it.

Whether it's through Lean, Six Sigma, or some other method, understanding the basics of process is a fundamental step on the road to Process Intelligence.

Follow a formal learning path for developing process knowledge. Define a maturity scale and appropriate targets, and implement a process training and education advancement program.

Applying process knowledge

After you learn the basics, you can apply process knowledge across your business world. For any process or activity, no matter how simple or complex, you can come to understand it and make it better.

> ✔ **Recognize** what a process looks like. Identify the suppliers and how the process works to transform inputs into outputs for the customer. Understand what information

and resources it needs. Learn how the process interacts with other processes in the bigger picture (the *value stream*).

✓ **Characterize** the process through measurement and analysis, in order to fully understand its behavior. Measure its performance and effectiveness and what it's truly capable of doing. Learn what influences it the most and the root causes of mistakes or wasted time.

Many people make the mistake of jumping directly to the step of designing improvements. You have to *measure first*. This way, you know precisely where you're starting from, and you'll be able to know later just how successful your changes are.

✓ **Identify ways you can improve the process.** How can you make it more effective at creating value? If necessary, run experiments or simulations to be sure.

✓ **Implement the improvements.** This can get complicated because it involves changing how people work. You may want to do this in small pockets or pilot areas and check how effective your improvements really are. Then you can make adjustments to be sure everyone will know how to act in the new ways.

✓ **Maintain the improved process.** Regularly measure and check the KPIs and provide feedback to everyone involved so they can keep the process performing to your expectations.

To be sure you have appropriate KPIs, use the SMART method:

✓ **Specific:** KPIs must be clear and specific, and call for specific actions and behaviors.

✓ **Measurable:** KPIs must be measurable and their improvement traceable.

✓ **Achievable:** The target KPI improvement values must be achievable; it must be possible to effectively change the root causes of the process behavior.

✓ **Relevant:** The KPIs must reflect the objectives.

✓ **Time-based:** Identify the valid time period for the KPIs and achieve the target KPI values within the specified period of time.

If you're an IT professional, chances are at this point you're thinking about just how much technology can assist in the world of process improvement. However, none of the basics of applied process knowledge necessarily require technology, and methods like Lean and Six Sigma don't specify technology. But without the power of technology, these methods are necessarily limited. That's why you have to combine the methods with technology to create Process Intelligence.

From Knowledge to Intelligence

After you learn the basics about process and how to apply your knowledge to improve processes, then you're ready to use tools and technologies to transform that knowledge into Process Intelligence. You need to implement the Process Intelligence technologies and then learn how to use them.

Implement the technologies of Process Intelligence as a strategic platform of technical capabilities, according to the information architecture defined in Chapter 3. You can implement each element of the Process Intelligence architecture to the extent necessary to fulfill immediate needs. Because the Process Intelligence architecture is part of a BPM suite and is based on SOA, you can start small and scale each functional element quickly as you need more capability.

Implementing Process Intelligence Technology

Follow a structured approach to implement Process Intelligence technology in four phases: strategy, design, implementation, and control.

Strategy phase

In the *strategy phase,* you begin cataloging the scope of your Process Intelligence deployment by identifying all the strategic, tactical, and operational processes (see Chapter 1 for more on this topic) you intend to manage as well as the associated business segment objectives and process KPIs. Store these definitions in a managed repository, where you can access them for analysis and later reuse. Answer these questions:

- ✔ What KPIs need to be measured — at all levels: strategic, tactical, and operational?
- ✔ What is the organizational structure around all the selected processes?
- ✔ Which processes will require detailed end-to-end examination?

Use *critical-to* (CT) analysis to identify the critical influencers on your KPIs. This helps you connect global corporate objectives to project and operational objectives.

CTs are those limited few activities that must be right in order to ensure successful process KPIs. They are the most influential areas *critical to* successful outcomes. CTs are as important to measure and manage as are the KPIs. You can relate these through a Cause and Effect (C&E) matrix.

Although your immediate effort may be focused around current problems with a specific transaction, workflow, or task, the overall improvement goal is often aimed at something larger (such as: *deliver a faster and better customer contact experience*). You must always be looking at the bigger picture and asking yourself where this task fits in the greater process, or value stream. You want to first have a good definition of the end-to-end process (such as: *contact-to-order*), so you can properly situate the specific task at hand.

Create a business segment matrix (BSM) to help you understand and organize the KPIs for a top management dashboard at a later time.

Design phase

In the *design phase,* translate the scope of the processes you identified in the strategy phase into detailed definitions. Include the elements needed in your Process Intelligence platform and supporting organization structures across your IT landscape. You're seeking to answer these questions:

- ✔ For our KPIs and CTs, what data do we need from which operational IT systems?

✔ What processing and analyses do we need to perform?

✔ What dashboard display structures do we need — at all three levels?

✔ What reporting schemas are appropriate?

Begin by dividing processes into sections, corresponding to a specific step of the process and the data needed in real time to characterize each state of the process at that step. Then identify the Process Intelligence elements (KPIs, CTs, analyses, reports, and dashboard entries) you need to support that step. For each KPI, use this checklist:

✔ **Description:** How is the KPI described?

✔ **Objective:** Which objective can this KPI measure?

✔ **Owner:** Who is responsible for ensuring the KPI's performance?

✔ **Business segment:** Which business segment is this KPI assigned to?

✔ **Unit of measure:** What is the unit of measure for this KPI?

✔ **Target mean value**: What value should be the mean, or average value?

✔ **Specification limits:** What range of values is within specification?

✔ **Alarm values:** What values should trigger an early-alert mechanism?

✔ **Formula:** How is this KPI calculated?

✔ **Frequency:** How often should this KPI be calculated?

✔ **Data source(s):** Where is the data coming from?

✔ **Data owner(s):** Who is responsible for the data delivery?

✔ **Measurement points:** Where are the data collection points within the processes?

✔ **Evaluations (dimensions):** By which criteria could the KPI be evaluated?

As you move through each process step, you will build up the set of intelligence elements needed to cover each process from the point of view of each of the three business levels (strategic, tactical, and operational). Also, for each business segment, identify and connect the relationships between KPIs and the process measurement points back to the business segment objectives (See Figure 4-1).

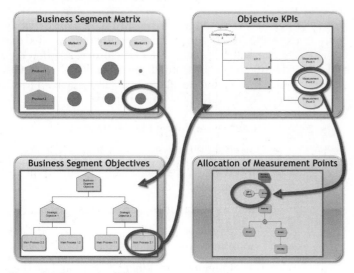

Figure 4-1: Connecting KPIs to measurement points.

Implementation phase

In the *implementation phase,* you produce an initial validated and integrated Process Intelligence platform that meets the scope and design.

A Process Intelligence platform, being SOA-based, is naturally scalable.

The first step in the implementation phase is to extract data for the periods, quantities, and times necessary, and per the time intervals you need to transfer data to the Process Intelligence platform.

After the Process Intelligence platform is operational, it will collect data automatically by continuously logging and measuring the running processes, performing the analytical processing, and populating the displays. See an example in Figure 4-2. With the platform in place, everyone can begin building the complete knowledge base they need to deliver real-time intelligence information on the quality, capability, and effectiveness of their processes.

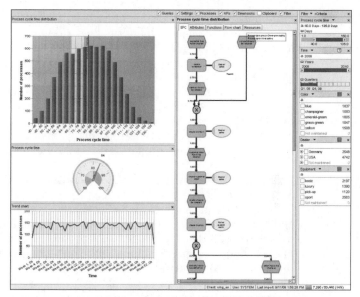

Figure 4-2: The Process Intelligence platform integrated histograms and run charts with visual process models.

Control phase

In the *control phase,* everyone will want to evaluate how well they're achieving their goals. They'll be looking at their dashboards and reports, and will be trying to figure out how well they can identify weaknesses in their record process flows and how effectively they can use their intelligence to lead to improvements. Process Intelligence software facilitates understanding of the actual step-by-step workflows in graphical process models, which in turn makes it easier to identify best practices (see Figure 4-2).

During the control phase, you'll hear these types of questions:

✔ Which performance variations are we highlighting?

✔ What organizational factors are influencing process performance?

✔ How do I create a permanent optimization loop?

✔ How does the IT system itself behave in the relevant production environment?

Periodically evaluate the contents and capabilities of your Process Intelligence platform. Be sure your Process Intelligence staff is getting all the capabilities and capacity they need. Typically, people want lots of slice-and-dice options for analyzing the content of all business data stored in a process warehouse, including ease of mining, integrated process benchmarking, and displaying individual and cumulative process instances. The calculated process data can be used in review workshops and reporting rounds to operationally enhance the end-to-end scenarios under examination.

Use Organizational Analysis (OA) to include organizational network factors that could influence process performance. This is a scientific method that will generate communication and activity charts. Use team meetings and workshops to help you correctly interpret the results. After you learn the process methods and techniques and you work with your IT organization to implement the Process Intelligence platform, you must also learn how to use the technologies. Be sure to make these part of your training regimen.

Chapter 5

Process Intelligence in Action

*T*his chapter takes a peek at what Process Intelligence can do in action. This is just a start, but it shows you the power of what's possible.

Follow along with the story of the sales managers for the fictional automobile manufacturer we call United Motors Group. Despite its brand prowess and reputation for quality, United Motors Group is facing challenges amid the rapidly changing market environment and global financial crisis. The Executive Board has implemented a strategy that includes process improvements. Managers across UMG are now defining and improving business processes.

Sales Challenges at UMG

Sales management at United Motors is dealing with several major challenges. The company's management team had conducted working sessions to identify programs that will boost performance. Three recommended strategies are:

✔ **Optimize and expand the product portfolio.** UMG wants to remain competitive as a market leader, so they're introducing new models, including a crossover, a hybrid green model, and a new small sports car. In addition, they're revamping their classic compacts and sedans (see Figure 5-1).

✔ **Reduce inventory costs.** The company is re-engineering its build-to-order processes and implementing shared-platform designs in order to reduce the parts in stock as well as the number of cars in inventory. This process re-engineering includes a glitzy new online *car configurator* for sales offices and online direct sales that UMG hopes will improve quality and reliability in the order process. A new supply chain optimization program seeks to improve procurement processes and the integration of external suppliers.

✔ **Boost sales efficiency and product turnover.** UMG will pursue new international market segments by addressing new customer target groups and open additional sales offices. They will discontinue unprofitable models. And they will look for improvements in the sales process.

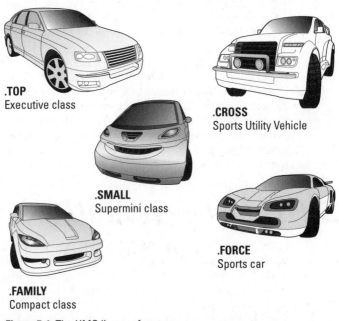

.TOP
Executive class

.CROSS
Sports Utility Vehicle

.SMALL
Supermini class

.FORCE
Sports car

.FAMILY
Compact class

Figure 5-1: The UMG lineup of cars.

In response, the sales team will improve the order processes and build up a sales performance management system based on key sales performance indicators. They want to have a process-oriented performance measurement system with early alerts and derived actions and be able to measure the processing time and quality in sales order processes. They have committed themselves to a program of continuous performance improvement.

Sales Process Intelligence at UMG

Seeking Process Intelligence, the sales team begins by identifying the strategic objectives and strategic KPIs. Then, they discover the existing processes and identify the associated operational KPIs. For example, the tactical KPI of *delivery reliability* leads the analysis of the order process to the operational KPIs *Order Process Cycle Time, Processing Time,* and *Changes Per Order.*

The sales team makes sure that everybody has the same understanding and agrees on the KPIs.

Following the measure-first approach, the team then baselines the sales order process by applying Process Intelligence to the ERP system that runs sales order processing. Their Process Intelligence reveals all the relevant process steps and information by reassembling each process instance, making everything visible, and revealing the KPIs, which are then available for dimensioning and analysis.

The process steps, associated KPIs, and dimensions are listed in Figure 5-2.

The KPIs and dimensions are for the most relevant CT *(critical-to)* metrics: the ones that most influence the process outcomes.

After automating the measurements, the team is able to capture order information every day. They implement sales dashboards that show the KPIs. See the example sales dashboard in Figure 5-3. Notice that the Sales Order Management Process tracks the KPIs from the delivery reliability analysis.

Process Steps	KPIs	Dimensions
Create quotation	Number of changes	Time
Create contract	Number of processes	Dealer
Create customer order	Process cycle time	Equipment
Create invoice	Processing time	Assembly location
Perform change on time	Time of contract to delivery	Order
Create delivery	Time of contract to invoice	Production location
Change customer order	Time of delivery to confirm receipt dealer	Product
Perform price change	Time of delivery to post goods issue	
Create pick order & shipping element		
Post goods issue		
Confirm goods receipt		
Deliver to customer		

Figure 5-2: The process steps, KPIs, and dimensions for the Sales Process.

Keep dashboards simple; don't make them too complex. Keep the number of KPIs down to what's critical. Also keep the navigations simple. You want dashboards to be easy for everyone to use.

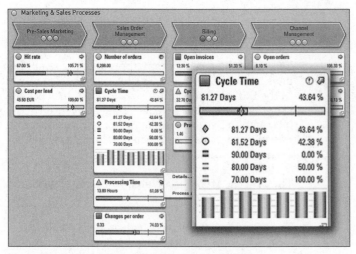

Figure 5-3: A sales dashboard; Cycle Time is highlighted.

Your first round of analysis usually reveals obvious opportunities for improvement. Typically, these improvements are straightforward and involve changes in procedure or behavior — not technology — per the Kaizen principle of *simplify and eliminate before you automate and integrate.*

From symptom to root cause

Seeing the sales process data in a dashboard gives the team immediate insight into process performance. For example, the dashboard reveals trouble with the sales process cycle time. The average cycle time of nearly 82 days is far above the target value of 70 days.

The dashboard reveals the issue. But what's causing it, and what should the team change in their process or in the organization to improve the cycle time?

The sales team uses Process Intelligence technology to analyze the relationships between KPIs, dimensions, and process structures. The first step in the analysis is in seeing the process cycle time distribution. See Figure 5-4. Just looking at the distribution, it's obvious that many orders are taking far too long. And yet, many are happening fast enough.

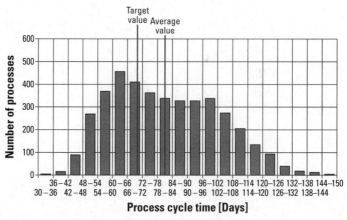

Figure 5-4: The distribution of process cycle time.

Across over 4,000 process instances, the first thing the team sees is that the range spans from a low of 36 days to a high of nearly 150 days. It's clear that the sales process is easily capable of meeting the 70-day target, but more often is just as likely to take up to 100 days or more. And they can just imagine what it's costing them when the process takes twice as long as it should!

But what's causing the bad process behavior? With Process Intelligence, it's easy to find out. The team simply examines instances of high versus low performance. Process Intelligence technology enables the two processes to be displayed as an Event-driven Process Chain (EPC).

Now, comparing good and bad performing sales processes is easy. The first EPC shows the good process: when the range is performing with a cycle time between 36 and 60 days. The bad process EPC is generated for cases where the process is over 100 days. The two are displayed side by side in Figure 5-5. The structure of the good process is slim and straightforward as it should be.

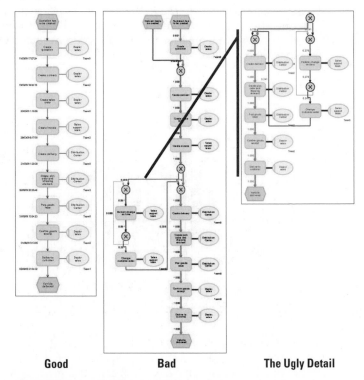

| Good | Bad | The Ugly Detail |

Figure 5-5: Automatic discovered process structures for sales orders. Detail reveals nature of poor process.

It's obvious immediately that the bad process has a branch and large loop of additional activity. No wonder those kinds of processes take longer! The reason for the bad performance is revealed when the team looks into the ugly details of the structure. There are order changes: In particular the process activity *Change Customer Order* is executed more than 40 percent of the time.

So the reason for the bad performance has been revealed, and the solution is in reducing the number of changes and modifications in an order. This will increase the process performance cycle time. The team can now concentrate on options for reducing order changes and immediately see the results of their improvements.

Where are the best practices?

Where are the best practices within teams or regions? And what are best practicers doing differently? The team analyzes the relationship between process performance and the joint work of departments and teams. Process Intelligence technology makes it easy: Instead of looking at the process structure, examine the organizational structure (see Figure 5-6).

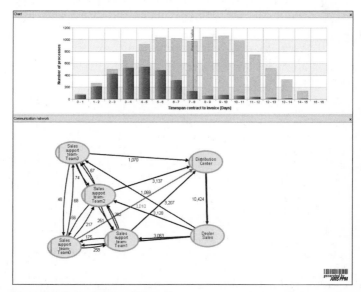

Figure 5-6: Best practice of Team 0.

Organization visualizations show the organizational units as connected nodes. The lines represent the transition of work in processes between organizational units. Notice the line from Team 0 of sales support to Distribution Center; its value of 3010 shows that Team 0 processed 3,010 sales orders and passed them to the distribution center team. That's roughly the same number as Teams 1 (3,128) and 2 (3,137) and nearly three times the volume of Team 3 (1,070).

Now link the behavior of each team with their process performance. Selecting the connecting line immediately displays the contribution of that relationship to the overall performance as the upper chart in the figure. In the example, you can clearly see that when Team 0 is involved, the cycle time is much lower. What is Team 0 doing differently? Using the Process Intelligence techniques, you can baseline the process instances of Team 0 and compare them with the other teams, as in Figure 5-5. In particular, if all other sales teams would adopt the best practices of Team 0, the average time span could be reduced dramatically! There is no need to implement new applications or processes; it is simply a matter of educating the other teams to use the knowledge that already exists within the organization.

Use your Process Intelligence to link KPIs to process execution to make their interdependence visible and actionable.

Chapter 6

Ten Application Scenarios for Process Intelligence

*T*his chapter gives you a look at some real-world application scenarios for Process Intelligence.

Contact-to-Order

A sales manager's main task is to advance a sales opportunity from lead-generation through to closing the deal. More than anything, the sales manager seeks transparency. Process Intelligence in the contact-to-order process supports an organization's process-oriented selling. The intelligence information doesn't imply additional effort by the sales staff because the necessary data is usually available directly from the company's CRM and other related systems. Along with KPI calculations for the entire process or for sub-processes, process-oriented analysis of quotation processing offers an early warning system for problems and supports internal auditing as well as customer-auditing functionality.

You can enable simple investigation into individual quotes and orders from aggregated views of activity by region or market because Process Intelligence integrates the operational and strategic levels. For example, you can link lead management, opportunity management, contract conclusion, invoicing, and commission sub-processes. You can also analyze by industry, region, time, and sales type for key indicators such as:

- ✔ Forecast value
- ✔ Incoming order value
- ✔ Opportunity-to-order time
- ✔ Conversion rate
- ✔ Forecast accuracy

Procure-to-Pay

The procurement-to-payment process handles the purchasing functions of a company. This includes originating and approving purchase orders, receiving and verifying the invoice and order, returns processing, and paying the bill. As more companies seek to move beyond procurement into fully deployed supply chain systems, a key challenge is in the area of improving efficiency in the procure-to-pay cycle. In this context, the supplier is also critical to the effectiveness of the process.

With Process Intelligence, you can have holistic and continuous reporting and analysis of the core processes across enterprises, as well as the presentation of decision-relevant information for different functional stakeholders within an enterprise. Process Intelligence enables:

- ✔ Support for strategic as well as operational decisions within the procurement-to-pay area
- ✔ Knowing the scope-of-delivery of the current top suppliers (over time and per segment)

> ✔ Understanding what improvements are possible by replacing poor-performing suppliers
>
> ✔ Discovering the main suppliers with insufficient adherence to delivery dates
>
> ✔ Visibility into performance against the service level agreements

Order-to-Cash

Optimizing order processing involves business processes with multiple interfaces to partners, customers, and logistics service providers. Due to the high number of interfaces, these processes are particularly error-prone: Experience shows that more than 25 percent of all such processes are inefficient; credit checks alone delay the completion of transactions. Although cost-reduction is a strategic goal for many organizations, the extra work involved in resolving process problems often actually *increases* costs. Managers are faced with the dilemma of reducing costs while at the same time deploying additional staff to ensure smooth execution of sales and logistics processes.

Process Intelligence reveals opportunities for savings by creating a transparent view of the entire process flow, including the interfaces (such as to credit bureaus). Automatic alerts when errors occur in the process flow save employees the time-consuming effort of trying to pin down problems. Weaknesses in individual process areas (such as sales, procurement, inventory, transport, invoicing, returns, and complaints) are highlighted and the potential for improvements is identified. KPIs for sales, quality, time, profit margin, service levels, and the associated causes of errors ensure that a high level of process quality is maintained at all times.

Process Intelligence is particularly helpful when you're managing the critical cycle times within an order process. Figure 6-1 shows example time spans you can see and manage when seeking to improve sales order processes.

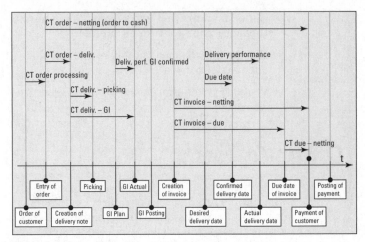

Figure 6-1: Time spans within an order-to-cash process.

Problem-to-Resolution

Service management focuses most directly on process quality, as measured by the performance to service level agreements (SLAs). Although SLAs tend to be highly customer-specific, they're also very time-critical, particularly around incident management. If a live system or facility fails, a response is required typically within minutes — or faster. To avoid penalties, businesses are constantly monitoring critical system and facility activities and managing problem scenarios, such as an unexpectedly high call-volume. Timely, automatic analysis and execution of ticket-handling processes is essential. A typical Process Intelligence solution provides a real-time dashboard that brings together key information, like:

- ✔ **Current Tasks:** Risks in current live processes require an immediate response.

- ✔ **Current Status:** A transparent view into process execution and visibility into unexpected behavior.

Logistics — Order Processing

Faced with ever-changing market conditions and business relationships, organizations are pressured to improve their logistics processes. Logistics innovations are being driven in particular by international competition in the transport sector. As logistics requirements become increasingly complex and global, organizations must remain flexible, which means ensuring transparent goods movements and efficient utilization of transport capacity. Handling orders that span multiple transport areas is a core logistics process.

Process Intelligence enables an integrated, cross-system view and analysis throughout the logistics chain, from order-entry to goods-movements and invoicing. Important quality-related supply chain KPIs include:

- ✔ The number of order changes

- ✔ Pickup compliance

- ✔ Cost (such as cost per order, cost per shipment)

- ✔ Time (such as time required for order entry, elapsed time between loading and departure, and so on)

- ✔ A compound metric, such as DIFOT (delivered in-full *and* on time)

Process Intelligence in the logistics sector yields a host of other benefits, including:

- ✔ Managing the supply chains for major customers using defined KPIs and SLAs

- ✔ SLA monitoring and benchmarking across transport companies and customers

- ✔ Proactive, timely response to early-warning conditions that affect KPIs and SLAs

- ✔ Improving customer service and quality through special automated reports on elapsed times, quantities, and SLA compliance

- ✔ Identifying optimization potential within the transport chain

Process Intelligence in Financials

Financial institutions use Process Intelligence in three main areas:

- ✔ Increase customer satisfaction, quality, and margins
- ✔ Lower the cost of compliance activities and improve the reliability of such activities
- ✔ Reduce and prevent risk

Process Intelligence crosses three disciplines: performance management, compliance management, and risk management. Executive organizations benefit from Process Intelligence, including the Chief Operating Officer (COO), who is responsible for operational results and the quality of processes; the Chief Financial Officer (CFO), who is responsible for financial results and rendering accounts to interested parties and shareholders; and the Chief Risk Officer (CRO), who is the conscience of the bank and responsible for saying no at the right moment and protecting the bank from risk.

Finally, there is a large group of professionals whose work is made easier from a financial, economic, and risk standpoint, including controllers, accountants, auditors, risk managers, compliance officers, process managers, quality managers, and business analysts.

Transaction Banking

Transaction banks execute large volumes of fast processes. Processing delays represent a significant financial risk and can damage their corporate image. Moreover, transactions are subject to stringent regulatory requirements. Manual tracking of enterprise-wide processes is difficult to implement at the transaction level, but short response times are vital in order to resolve bottlenecks and problems with minimum delay.

At the business process level, real-time, event-driven process monitoring offers a reliable way of automatically monitoring the status of all current transactions. Your Process

Intelligence tools include fully automated, rule-based correlation filters that respond to specific patterns in the event streams of the IT systems with an immediate warning. These exceptions are reported immediately to the process manager, who can quickly take the necessary corrective action before a bottleneck causes problems.

This automated process monitoring minimizes the risk of payment system failures and increases process efficiency because every transaction that deviates from the norm is identified. The Process Intelligence solution becomes a permanent, real-time early warning system that ensures that all live business processes are transparent and of a consistently high quality.

Straight-Through Processing

Straight-through processing (STP) is how companies achieve an uninterrupted flow of transactions. STP demands that you handle high transaction rates and respond quickly to exceptions. Process best practices will suggest you reduce system complexity. STP will help you shorten throughput times, reduce risk, improve predictability, and lower operating costs. You'll strive to avoid manual interventions because they lead to reduced efficiencies and greater risks. Process Intelligence will tell you which situations require manual intervention. Also, for banks that outsource some of their processes to third parties, straight-through processing is an excellent tool for testing compliance with agreed standards.

Risk and Compliance

Reconstructing an actual process from end to end provides an ideal source of information for anticipating what will follow. You can immediately identify open positions, deviant transactions, and processes that fail to run as agreed. This reconstruction also ties together the requirements for demonstrable compliance contained in such legislation and regulations as Sarbanes-Oxley, Basel II, and WFT, as well as being useful when implementing corporate governance. It makes it easier for banks to present the monitored process behavior to an auditor in order to demonstrate proper process management and implementation of the necessary control measures. The visualizations provide immediate answers to process and organizational questions, such as:

- Who did what and when did they do it?
- Is there proper separation of duties?
- Are people adhering to agreements?
- Are procedures being followed?

Visualization of the actual process paths serves as the basis of evidence. In addition, Process Intelligence looks beyond the operational processes. A bank can also deploy visualization to examine the compliance process itself.

- Are we in control? Are we on schedule?
- Do we carry out our random surveys properly and on time?
- Who performed which audits and when?

Insurance

By continuously measuring and analyzing the efficiency of core processes, such as application management and claims handling, insurers achieve a competitive advantage.

Process Intelligence enables the automatic evaluation of real transactions in the underlying systems across the entire organization — beginning with insurance applications, through to signed contracts and claims management. This creates transparency along the value chain and uncovers hidden potential for efficiency savings. Successful insurers automatically measure and evaluate their actual business processes using operational KPIs, such as throughput times (from new application to issuing the policy), or the process costs of transactions involving manual intervention.

Process Intelligence also reveals the underlying processes executed for every KPI, so process managers have insight into the conditions that give rise to repeated problems at any stage of processing.

Process Intelligence provides the flexibility for people to understand what's happening with individual transactions and single steps within a process. Process Intelligence also supports aggregating multiple processes into a single process. A complete picture of the entire process can be retained from beginning to end, and the causes of any material process problems can be revealed within the context of all participants.

Process Intelligence delivers the hard facts that force the line managers to accountability for their contribution to business success. At the same time, everyone involved in the process is accessing a current knowledge base in order to eliminate recurring process weaknesses within their departments before bad processes impact negatively on the bottom line.

Successful insurers develop Process Intelligence to slash wait times for new customers, boost the quality of instant decisions, and free up resources by reducing customer queries.

Chapter 7

Ten Best Practices of Process Intelligence

*H*ere are ten best practices to keep in mind as you develop your Process Intelligence.

Get Process Savvy

You can only unleash the power of Process Intelligence if you know your process stuff. You have to have process savvy to wield Process Intelligence. Process Intelligence isn't something that comes out of a box. You don't just plug it in and turn it on. To have great influence, you need to learn and understand the fundamentals of process.

Build a structure for Business Process Management and seek to create a culture of business process excellence. Learn the methods and tools of process improvement. Educate people at all levels and across all functions of the business.

Create Value

You can have all the Process Intelligence in the world, but if you don't use it to create value, you're just wasting your time. Process Intelligence exists to see where more value can be created. This is why KPIs are *key*. Use your Process

Intelligence for good in the world by finding waste, errors, and defects and helping create better ways of working that add customer value and create more benefit for you and your business.

Engage the Stakeholders

Process Intelligence can be a weapon. Because knowledge is power, people will fear its power unless you have the trust and confidence of the stakeholders. You need to enroll the people who are most affected and have the most to gain or lose by the power of Process Intelligence. At all three levels (strategic, tactical, and operational) Process Intelligence has an impact. Across all areas of business and within the technology arena, Process Intelligence has an impact. Engage stakeholders across these domains. Ensure that key people see the benefits and will embrace the opportunities.

Establish the Wellspring of Knowledge

People are naturally baffled by the many new competencies and technologies involved in Process Intelligence. The best way to facilitate easy adoption and understanding is by establishing a formal way to learn and apply the skills and tools of Process Intelligence. This wellspring of knowledge should include methods and best practices. People should have easy access to training and skills, mentoring, and help. You want to apply program and project management practices as well as agile development methods. Be sure to include any Lean or Six Sigma training. Although some enterprises establish a formal competency center or center of excellence for Process Intelligence, others establish virtual centers. The degree of formality isn't so important; it's the degree of knowledge that counts.

Intelligence Is for Everyone

Process Intelligence isn't a specialty. It's for everybody — at all levels — who performs any function within processes across the enterprise. The level of versatility will vary across your business, and adoption will naturally occur in pockets.

But don't think that Process Intelligence should be confined to just a few special people. Everyone works in processes, so everyone benefits from Process Intelligence. You'll be surprised by who steps forward and wants to learn and apply Process Intelligence. Whoever they are, be sure to support them: They're the ones developing the capability to improve your business.

Make sure that everyone understands that Process Intelligence is a special gift that anyone can use. Be sure to share it with people and evangelize its value.

Use process visualizations as you communicate in your business relationships — they're exciting and effective! Advertise the value created when Process Intelligence improves business performance. Facilitate the sharing of knowledge and best practices.

Measure First

Before ever taking action to change a process or activity, be sure to measure and characterize the as-is process first. Just like you want your doctor to thoroughly diagnose your ailment before recommending a treatment, you want to measure and characterize a "sick" business process before prescribing the improvements. As the saying goes, you can't manage what you don't measure. Intelligence is based on knowledge, which comes from observation and measurement. Process Intelligence means you've measured your processes. Use all the tools of collection and processing, including process discovery and activity monitoring, and always measure in terms of strategic and operational KPIs.

Keep Things Simple

Einstein is famously quoted as saying we should keep things "as simple as possible — but not simpler." Apply this rule to Process Intelligence.

You can imagine how complicated processes and measurements and analyses can become. And complex problems sometimes demand complex answers. But the real value in Process Intelligence is to gain the insight needed to pinpoint the simple things that can have significant effect. You'll lose everyone if you make it too complicated, make the projects too big, and prolong the results. Use your Process Intelligence wisely, and keep it simple.

Sync Up with Strategy

In applying your Process Intelligence, be sure to check the alignment of individual process performances and behaviors with your enterprise or corporate strategy. The flow-down of strategy into tactical and operational processes works in reverse, too: Operational processes should support tactical objectives and strategic goals. Strategic objectives can be expressed as KPIs, and these can be flowed down such that even the lowest operational processes are connected to them. Process Intelligence is very powerful this way. You can directly facilitate the alignment of everyday work to strategic goals.

SOA It Goes

When it comes to the technologies for Process Intelligence, remember that Process Intelligence isn't a "package" or "an application" that you buy and implement. Process Intelligence technologies are a suite of capabilities deployed within a Service Oriented Architecture. This means that the technology for Process Intelligence can be developed in segments and layers, starting small and scaling over time.

Intelligence Is Forever

As time moves forward, things change. Even a process that's perfect today won't be so perfect tomorrow. Markets, competition, innovation, resources, technology, variation, wear — they all conspire to degrade performance or effectiveness. Process Intelligence is your view into these changes. It's how you'll always stay aware. Developing and maintaining this capability is how you'll always be a step ahead.

Chapter 8

Ten Process Intelligence Pitfalls to Avoid

In This Chapter

▶ Avoiding the most common mistakes

▶ Increasing your chances of success

*I*f you avoid these mistakes, you're bound to be successful with your Process Intelligence initiative.

Taking Your Eye Off the Ball

Process Intelligence can be a complex combination of applied knowledge and technology, and it includes many capabilities as well as technological features and components. It's easy to get caught up in the technologies and analytical capabilities and take your eye off the ball of generating business value. Remember that the purpose of Process Intelligence is to help you improve a process that increases performance and produces better business results. Don't wander off into starting big technology projects or get wrapped up in "analysis paralysis" or attempt to boil the ocean and solve all the world's problems. Solve the current issue now, and generate measurable value. It's one pitch at a time. Keep your eye on the ball.

Lonesome Cowboy

When you're pursuing support for infrastructure, tools, or training to establish your Process Intelligence capabilities, don't go it alone. Trying to herd the cattle all by yourself will make you one lonesome cowboy. With Process Intelligence, be sure to round up help — from both business people and IT specialists.

Without guidance from business people, you'll have trouble understanding how best to approach developing the capabilities and applying them where they're needed most. With no one to help keep you on track, you can find yourself out in the cold, and your efforts won't produce real business value or gain the endorsements of business leaders. Meanwhile, the same goes for assistance from the IT organization. You don't want to go the IT route alone, either. You want sponsorship and support in the IT community around the architecture and technology tool-sets of Process Intelligence.

We Already Have This

People have been creating reports and dashboards and implementing database query and business intelligence tools for years. Process quality engineers have been applying the tools of process control since the 1940s. Six Sigma has been around since 1981. You may find that people will look beyond the new and unique capabilities of Process Intelligence and say, "We already have this."

No, they don't. They may have bits and pieces, and there may be very talented and experienced individuals around, but Process Intelligence is a new capability. It's partly a combination of existing methods, tools, and technologies, but it's a new way of assembling and using these that's well beyond the old ways in terms of the level of insight, ease of use, speed of response, and transparency. As a result, it creates more value.

 Process Intelligence is more responsive, more scalable, more integrated, and more valuable than anything that's come before.

It's an IT Thing

Because Process Intelligence strongly leverages technology, it naturally involves the technology community. Also, because Process Intelligence technologies are so powerful, they naturally come to the forefront of attention. In addition, because the tools are so powerful and easy to use, the IT community supports the hands-on involvement and use of Process Intelligence technology by the business community. As a result, Process Intelligence is often introduced into the enterprise by the technology community and therefore is seen as "an IT thing." Once this happens, Process Intelligence initiatives can easily be viewed within the enterprise as technology projects.

For all you technologists out there excited about the prospects of Process Intelligence in your organization, be very careful to avoid having Process Intelligence perceived as a technology-based initiative. You have a role in facilitating the SOA connections and components, in installing and configuring tools, and in learning to apply the methods and techniques. But Process Intelligence isn't IT. Process Intelligence is a business value generator. Be sure to keep it oriented as a business tool, focused on business processes and improving business performance.

It's a Secret Weapon

You can't be afraid of transparency and of sharing what you know. If you treat Process Intelligence as something that's a secret weapon only for the chosen few, you inhibit its reach and value. And if you're afraid that the visibility and results will imply changes that no one will accept, you're defeating yourself and your business.

Process Intelligence is for everyone, at all levels across the enterprise, and with it they will create visibility and transparency about processes that aren't working well. Don't hide from this. An underperforming process is an opportunity to make things better and make more money.

You Forgot the K in KPI

Lots of things can be indicators of performance, but they're not necessarily the *key* indicators that are critical to quality, value, and improved performance. Don't forget that the *K* in KPI stands for *key*. When you instrument a process, you don't want to measure all the indicators of performance, or just your favorite indicators, or the ones that are easiest to measure, or even the indicators that everyone has traditionally measured, because these aren't necessarily the key indicators of process performance.

As the saying goes, "Be careful what you measure, because that's what you're going to improve." If you measure the wrong things, you're going to get the wrong answers and subsequently take the wrong actions. The best tools and visibility in the world don't help if you're measuring the wrong thing. Be sure you analyze your processes to determine which performance indicators are *truly* key to what matters most: process quality, value-stream effectiveness, and customer satisfaction. Measure those.

Baaad Data

"Garbage in, garbage out." All the processing and visualization aren't going to give you a good answer if you're processing bad data. Bad data leads to bad intelligence. Be careful that you ensure the quality of data on which you base your intelligence. You'll encounter special challenges when you have to combine data from different sources. Fortunately, there are many tools and techniques available for detecting bad data and taking action. Include these in your Process Intelligence portfolio.

Measure Everything!

Once people understand the power of Process Intelligence, you'll find that many become so fascinated that they try to measure every step in every task and every minor subtask, believing that infinite measurement to infinitesimal detail is the basis of process quality and performance improvement. It's a common mistake to apply more measuring points and more KPIs in the belief that more is better.

In fact, more isn't better. It's just more. Which is more effort to collect, to process, to qualify, to analyze, and to manage. And it's unnecessary because you only need to measure the key influencers on process performance. Just measure what's necessary.

IT Doesn't Know Process

Historically, the business and operations staff have learned and applied the methods and techniques of process improvement. It's traditionally not been taught to the IT staff. Very few IT professionals are Six Sigma Black Belts or Lean Masters, for example. As a result, the IT community, by and large, isn't familiar or conversant, let alone expert, with these methods and techniques. This has fostered a general belief that IT doesn't know process. And misunderstandings between the IT and business communities tend to arise around process improvement and BPM.

Try to get the IT community up to speed with the business community on process. IT folks need to know and practice the process improvement methods that are now so broadly used in the business communities. IT people need to see processes in a business context so they can better understand the processing and visualization needs of Process Intelligence.

Being Scatterbrained

By now you should know that Process Intelligence is a discipline. It's not a tool, or a software application, or a computer screen or button you can press, or a dial you can turn. And hopefully by now you also know that Process Intelligence is a discipline that's connected to how you run your business and manage work.

As a discipline, Process Intelligence requires that you be focused, thorough, and professional in how you apply the methods and tools. You can't be scatterbrained about it or it won't come together, and people won't be able to make sense of your processes or improve your business. Establish a basis of competency and governance in how you manage Process Intelligence. Your business processes are proprietary intellectual property, and the KPIs you manage are, in fact, enterprise assets, which should be maintained and controlled. It's a good idea to store process knowledge in a library and for the process services functions to be managed through your SOA initiative. In addition, Process Intelligence should be governed within your overall BPM management structure. Your Process Intelligence approach should be systematic.

Appendix A

Glossary

●●●

Automated Organizational Discovery: A re-engineering approach to automatically identify the relationships (for instance: delegates, collaborates) between the organizational items (for instance: people, teams, departments) of a company.

Automated Process Discovery: A re-engineering approach to automatically reconstruct models of process instances based on process-oriented information (process fragments) from different source systems. The aggregation of single process instances to a common visualization is part of Automated Process Discovery.

Balanced Scorecard: A framework for identifying business metrics beyond the basic financial measures normally used. Balanced Scorecards include customer, process, and people measures as well as financial information. They tie together strategic goals with operational metrics.

Benchmarking: The process of comparing business scenarios and identifying best practices by determining which is the very best. Benchmarking is usually part of a larger effort, such as a Process Re-engineering or Quality Improvement initiative.

BPM Suite (BPMS): A comprehensive software suite facilitating all aspects of Business Process Management, including process design, workflow, applications, integration, and activity monitoring for both system and human-centric environments.

Business Activity Monitoring (BAM): Software for the real-time monitoring of business processes.

Business Intelligence (BI): A general term for computer-based techniques for analyzing business data.

Business Performance Management (BPM): Often used synonymously with Corporate Performance Management (CPM), this is a metrics-based analysis of a company's operations and performance and is usually focused on the financial aspects.

Business Process Management (BPM): The methods, techniques, and tools used to design, enact, control, and analyze operational business processes involving people, systems, applications, data, and organizations.

Business Transformation: A business initiative that re-aligns people, process, and technology to achieve significant changes and improvements in performance through organizational change.

Complex Event Processing (CEP): Computing that performs on events, including capturing, creating, correlating, or transforming them with low latency to react in real time.

Continuous Process Improvement (CPI): An unceasing effort to discover and eliminate the causes of problems in the performance of business processes and increase value creation and productivity.

Corporate Performance Management (CPM): The metrics-based analysis of a company's current operations and performance, very often with a focus on the financial aspects. Often used synonymously with Business Performance Management (BPM).

Critical Success Factor (CSF): An element that is vital for a company's strategy to be successful. Typical examples are high product quality, low product cost, attracting the best personnel, strong brand image, and so on.

Cycle Time: The total elapsed time from the time a task, product, or service is started until it is completed.

Dashboard: A visual display that indicates the status or health of a business enterprise or process via numeric and graphical Key Performance Indicators.

Delivery Reliability: Ratio of the number of deliveries made without any error (regarding time, price, quantity, and quality) to the total number of deliveries in a period.

DMAIC: The acronym for the five core phases of the Six Sigma methodology: Define, Measure, Analyze, Improve, and Control; used to solve process and business problems through data and analytical methods.

Event-driven Architecture (EDA): An approach for the development of IT systems where the cooperation between the different components is triggered by events. Typically, an Event-driven Architecture relies on publishers and subscribers to achieve high flexibility and openness.

Event-driven Process Chain (EPC): A widespread notation for business process modeling.

Governance: A framework for decision and accountability that produces desirable outcomes within the organization. The governance framework determines the what, who, and how of enterprise decision-making.

Governance, Risk, and Compliance (GRC): Umbrella term covering an organization's approach to responding appropriately to risks and to conforming to legal requirements.

Key Performance Indicators (KPIs): Any set of financial or nonfinancial metrics that can be measured to quantify business performance. For example, process cycle time.

Mashup: The integration of information from different sources by using editors that allow the remix of data without programming.

Measure First: The practice of beginning a BPM project or initiative by first measuring the present state of a business process to establish a valid baseline.

Online Analytical Processing (OLAP): A technique of Business Intelligence to enable multidimensional queries using measures (for example: cost, cycle time) and dimensions (for example: region, period, product).

Organizational Analysis (OA): A methodology to identify the social relationships between the nodes (people, teams, departments, and so on) of a social network; the results are displayed in graph-based structures and social network diagrams.

Portal: A software framework that enables people, via a unitary interface provided through a Web browser, to manage information and processes across systems or organizations.

Predictive Analytics: Algorithms applied to patterns of information about activities and behaviors that serve as a statistically valid basis for predicting potential future outcomes.

Process: A set of activities, material, and/or information flow that transforms a set of inputs into defined outputs.

Process Instance: A single specific execution of a generic process type, for instance, the 4711th time the order-to-cash process was executed today, by a specific individual, with their activities and materials.

Process Intelligence (PI): The combination of analytical functionality and monitoring capabilities with process information to enable performance management on strategic, tactical, and operational levels.

Process Mining: A set of techniques to identify correlations within process data to identify bottlenecks and potential for optimization.

Process Model: A representative prescription for how a set of activities should operate in a sequential flow in order to regularly achieve desired outcomes.

Process Optimization: The practice of making changes and adjustments to a process in order to improve its efficiency or effectiveness.

Process Owner: The individual who has responsibility for process performance and resources and who provides support, resources, and functional expertise to projects. The process owner is accountable for implementing process improvements.

Root Cause Analysis: A category of problem-solving methods to analyze the origin of problems and to define corrective measures.

Service Level Agreement (SLA): The formal definition of a service level within a service contract between a customer and the service provider. SLAs are described by performance metrics to specify the levels of availability, serviceability, performance, and operation.

Service Oriented Architecture (SOA): A software architecture in which previously created features and functions can be leveraged and reused to quickly build new services.

Simulation: The computer modeling of a hypothetical example that can be analyzed to determine how a given application of systems may operate when deployed.

Six Sigma: A proven and proscriptive set of analytical tools, project control techniques, reporting methods, and management techniques that combine to form breakthrough improvements in problem-solving and business performance.

Supply Chain: The system of people, activities, information, and resources involved in the movement of a product or service from supplier to customer.

Appendix B

Resources

Web Resources

✔ www.processintelligencefordummies.com. Learn more about *Process Intelligence For Dummies* at the book's Web site. Take an interactive quiz of your process IQ and access other resources such as articles and Webinars.

✔ www.process-intelligence.com. Learn more about process intelligence and stay up-to-date on related news and events.

✔ www.processturnaround.com. Step through a detailed use case of how a company can leverage Process Intelligence for improved results with the fictional company, United Motor Group. Watch as the CEO and CIO of UMG explain how they optimized UMG's business using the Business Process Excellence Lifecycle.

✔ www.ariscommunity.com/aris-express. Model your business with ARIS Express. ARIS Express is the perfect tool for starting with Business Process Management and supports intuitive and fast process modeling. Recommended for beginners to experts.

✔ www.arisalign.com. Join the BPM social network ARISalign. You can model processes and share them with your colleagues. Build a network of other professionals working on the same problem and share the benefits of industry best practices.

✔ www.mashzone.com. Create informative dashboards in minutes with ARIS MashZone. You can use MashZone to create attractive business mashups to visualize operational metrics and much more.

✔ www.centrasite.org. Model your IT architecture using SOA Governance with CentraSite. Using CentraSite, you can manage the services that support your business processes and identify the impact of changes to your IT architecture.

✔ www.softwareag.com/performancedriven. Learn how your organization can become performance-driven. Access articles, Webcasts, and informative whiteboard videos to learn how customers are applying the concepts of Process Intelligence to become performance-driven.

Blogs and Community Forums

✔ The ARIS Community (www.ariscommunity.com) has discussion forums and articles on several Process Intelligence topics including BPM and Enterprise Architecture. Also check out the twitter feed at twitter.com/ariscommunity.

✔ Software AG's corporate blog (blog.softwareag.com) contains news and updates on Process Intelligence, BPM, and SOA. Also check out Software AG's twitter feed at twitter.com/SoftwareAG.

✔ Information Management (www.information-management.com/channels/business_process_management.html) maintains a channel of useful articles and books on BPM in general.

Books

For an introduction to the concepts of BPM and SOA, please look at the two previous books in this *For Dummies* series (www.softwareag.com/dummies):

✔ *BPM Basics For Dummies* by Kiran Garimella, Michael Lees, and Bruce Williams

✔ *SOA Adoption For Dummies* by Miko Matsumura, Bjoern Brauel, and Jignesh Shah

Other helpful *For Dummies* books include:

- *Six Sigma For Dummies* by Craig Gygi and Bruce Williams
- *Lean For Dummies* by Natalie Sayer and Bruce Williams

Conferences

- **Gartner BPM Summit** (www.gartner.com): See thought leaders, customers, and vendors; good for architects and business leaders.

- **Forrester Technology Leadership Forum** (www.forrester.com): See experts, case studies, and technologies in one location; good conference for all roles in the BPM initiative; a focus on strategy.

- **ProcessWorld** (www.processworld.com): Focused on practical strategies that organizations use to achieve process excellence.

Technology Vendors

Vendors have great knowledge and expertise. Of course, each has a perspective that's in its own interest, but they're betting their business on understanding what's right for the marketplace. Vendors want you to be informed and will spend marketing and sales money informing you.

Analyst Firms

The IT analyst firms employ some of the best BPM and BI expertise in the industry and provide independent advice to help you evaluate vendors and start planning BPM projects:

- **Gartner Research** (www.gartner.com): Covers a broad range of products and methodologies, along with an annual review of the vendor landscape.

- **Forrester Research** (www.forrester.com): Provides research and events on vendors and best practices, as well as annual reports on the top BPM vendors.

✔ **Burton Group** (www.burtongroup.com): Provides strong technical research and advisory services.

Look around You!

You have more resources around you than you may realize. Your co-workers may have experience in Business Process Management or Business Intelligence. You have business people in your IT organization and IT people in your business organization. You have champions and supporters of change and young people aggressively pursuing new approaches. Take advantage of your own network of experience and support.

Software AG

Software AG (www.softwareag.com) is a global leader in Business Process Excellence. Software AG brings you education, training, references, resources, world-class partners and consultants, and a fully integrated suite of products to implement Process Intelligence.